Eve and Adam
and their Very First Day

by Leslie Kimmelman

illustrated by Irina Avgustinovich

APPLES & HONEY PRESS

To Poppy, Asher, Izzy, Davy, and Willa,
the next generation of strong women. —L. K.

To Yan, my daily inspiration. Rejoice, be surprised and explore this life
like the first day in the Garden of Eden. —I. A.

This story is told using the ancient Jewish tradition of studying
and filling in the gaps of Bible stories called *midrash*.

Apples & Honey Press
An imprint of Behrman House
Millburn, New Jersey 07041
www.applesandhoneypress.com

Text copyright © 2023 by Leslie Kimmelman
Illustrations copyright © 2023 by Irina Avgustinovich

ISBN 978-1-68115-625-5

Library of Congress Cataloging-in-Publication Data

Names: Kimmelman, Leslie, author. | Avgustinovich, Irina, illustrator.
Title: Eve and Adam and their very first day / by Leslie Kimmelman ; illustrated by Irina Avgustinovich.
Description: Millburn : Apples & Honey Press, an imprint of Behrman House
[2023] | Audience: Ages 4-7. | Audience: Grades K-1. | Summary: Together Eve and Adam experience their first day--and night-- in the Garden of Eden.
Identifiers: LCCN 2022057972 | ISBN 9781681156255 (hardcover)
Subjects: LCSH: Eve (Biblical figure)--Juvenile fiction. | Adam (Biblical   figure)--Juvenile fiction. | Eden--Juvenile fiction. |
Creation--Juvenile fiction. | Faith--Juvenile fiction. | CYAC: Eve (Biblical figure)--Fiction. | Adam (Biblical figure)--Fiction. | Eden--Fiction.
| Creation--Fiction. | Faith--Fiction. | LCGFT: Religious fiction.
Classification: LCC PZ7.K56493 Ev 2023 | DDC 813.54 [E]--dc23/eng/20230214
LC record available at https://lccn.loc.gov/2022057972
Design by Jennifer Rinaldi
Edited by Aviva Lucas Gutnick
Printed in China

1 3 5 7 9 8 6 4 2

It was Eve's first day in the Garden of Eden.

Actually, it was her first day anywhere,

since she was newly created.

God had made her wonderfully well.

Eve was not afraid of anything.

She was not afraid of the wild
green tangle of the garden.
Not afraid of the tall leafy trees
soaring up into the sky.

Not afraid of the vivid, rainbow-colored
flowers growing all around her,
their sweet scents perfuming the air.

Not afraid of the brilliant ball
of yellow burning above her.
Not afraid of the fantastic creatures
leaping,
crawling,
climbing,
flying
everywhere.

And she was definitely not afraid of the friendly-looking two-legged creature standing right beside her.

He called himself Adam.

Adam had a beautiful smile.

He and Eve walked through the garden together, giving a name to each thing they saw.

"Oak," said Adam. "Cat. Dog. Ant."

Pretty boring, Eve thought.

She'd help Adam work on his imagination later.

Maybe it was because Adam had been first.
Eve came second, and, well, practice makes
perfect.

Okay, maybe not perfect, she thought modestly.
"Nightingale," she offered aloud. "Weeping
willow. Bumblebee. Nine-banded armadillo."
She touched something red and bumpy, with a
green hat on top.

"Strawberry," she added.

"You're really good at this," said Adam, smiling.
"Thank you," said Eve. She liked that Adam
was not only beautiful, but also kind.

Drip.

Something wet

fell on Eve's nose.

Drip.

On Adam's head.

On Eve's arm.

On Adam's toes.

Drip.

Drip.

Drip.

What was it?

Adam looked up.

"Rain," he decided.

"It's falling from that
gray shape in the sky."

The rain fell faster.

There was a booming noise and a bright flash.

"Thunder," Eve suggested. "And lightning."

Adam looked concerned. "It's loud. Do you think it's safe?"

Eve was not afraid.

"I don't think we should worry," she said.

"Whatever happens, we have God. We have each other. It will be all right."

And it was.

The rain stopped and the
yellow ball appeared again.
It s-t-r-e-t-c-h-e-d
its warmth and light over the garden.

Adam breathed deeply.
"It will be all right," he reminded himself.
He looked at the yellow ball carefully. "Sun?" he asked.
"And sunbeams?"
"Nice choices," replied Eve.

Eve and Adam discovered new miracles all day long.

The Garden of Eden was spectacular.

"This is the best day ever," said Eve.

Adam had to agree. "The first, and the best."

Until . . . the sun started to drop.

Adam noticed first.

"Um, Eve," he told her nervously, pointing upward.

"The sun is falling down."

"Surely not," replied Eve. "You must be imagining it."

But he wasn't imagining it.

The sun dropped down . . .

and down . . . and down . . .

and completely disappeared.

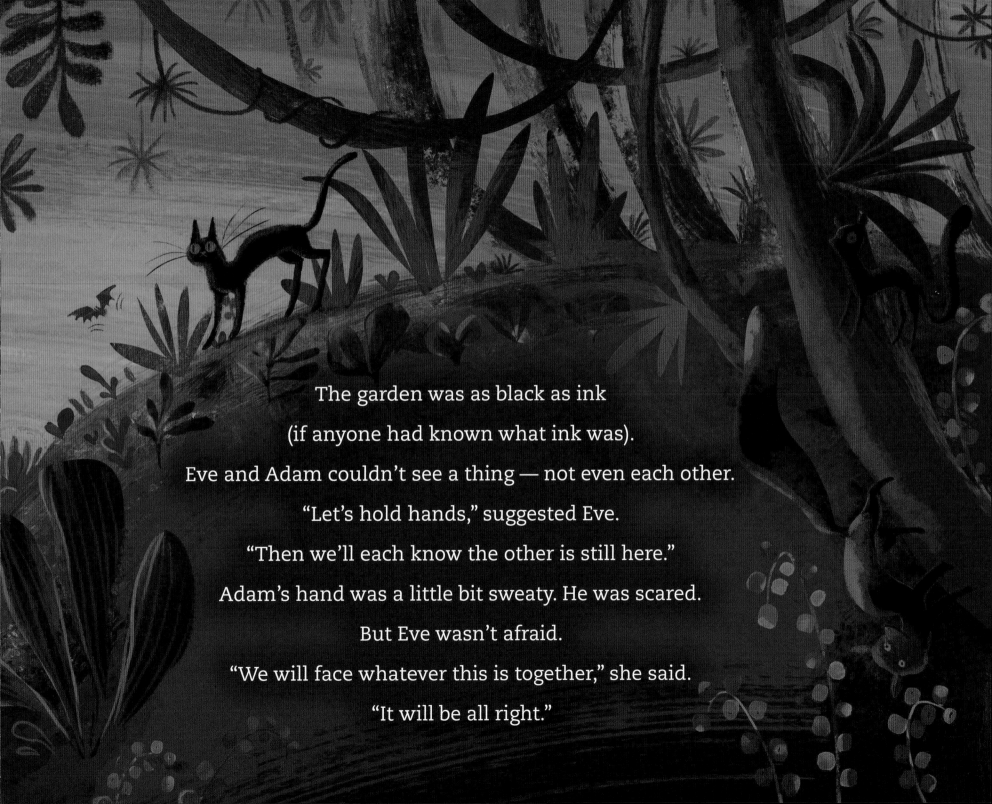

The garden was as black as ink

(if anyone had known what ink was).

Eve and Adam couldn't see a thing — not even each other.

"Let's hold hands," suggested Eve.

"Then we'll each know the other is still here."

Adam's hand was a little bit sweaty. He was scared.

But Eve wasn't afraid.

"We will face whatever this is together," she said.

"It will be all right."

Still, it was very dark

for a very,

very,

VERY long time.

"It will be all right?" Eve said again.

Her voice sounded a little nervous.

Eve wondered and worried.

Adam shook and shivered.

Then two amazing things happened.

First, thousands of tiny blinking lights

appeared all around them.

Second, thousands of tiny sparkles

appeared in the sky high above them.

"The sun has broken into millions
of pieces!" cried Adam in a panic.
"What will become of us?"
Eve had a different idea.
"I don't think so," she said.
"I think these, um, fireflies and those,
um, stars are a sign from God.
I think God is reminding us that
YOU ARE NOT ALONE.
HAVE FAITH."

So Eve and Adam kept hold of their faith.

They kept hold of each other's hands.

They fell fast asleep in the sweetly scented garden.

And when they woke up . . .

a new day had begun, a second day,

ordinary and miraculous.

The sun shone.

The birds sang.

Flowers opened and leaves unfurled.

And Eve and Adam saw that it was good.

Dear Readers,

Experiencing something new and not knowing what's going to happen next can be pretty scary. Can you imagine how it would feel to see the sun for the first time, as Eve and Adam did, and then see it disappear, not knowing if it would ever rise in the sky again?

That's where faith comes in. There are always going to be tough moments in life. But having faith—whether it's in yourself, in the people around you, or in God—helps make it easier to face whatever challenges come up.

May you have many beautiful sunrises and sunsets — and people you love to experience them with.

Leslie